SUN, MOON, SALT

SUN, MOON, SALT

Nancy White

*Winner of the 1992
Word Works Washington Prize*

THE WORD WORKS
WASHINGTON, DC

Second Edition
First Printing
Sun, Moon, Salt
Copyright © 1992, 2010 by Nancy White

Reproduction of any part of this book in any form or by any means, electronic or mechanical, including photocopying, must be with permission in writing from the publisher. Please address inquiries to:

The WORD WORKS
PO Box 42164,
Washington, DC 20015
editor@wordworksdc.com

Cover art "Frog" by Anastasia Nute
Author photo by Kirby Vaillant-White
Book design by Janice Olson

Printed in the United States by Lightning Source, Inc.

Library of Congress Number: 2009936389
International Standard Book Number: 978-0-915380-74-9

ACKNOWLEDGEMENTS

A number of poems in this book have appeared in the following journals:

Binnewater Tides, "Red or Clear," "The Red Angel," "The Teacher"; *Black Warrior Review,* "Confection"; *Cottonwood,* "Country Town"; *Exquisite Corpse,* "Look"; Feminist Studies, "Eve Leaves"; *FIELD,* "Eve's Garden"; *Massachusetts Review,* "Life of a Girl," "The Air They Breathe," "To My Sins"; *Puerto Del Sol,* "The Heart Is a Muscle"; *Ploughshares,* "Tongue," "Walking Down Court Street," "Winter," "The Function of Clouds," "Father on Black Ice," "When You Unloose"; *Quarry West,* "Blue Heron," "Pickles"; *Seattle Review,* "Sleep of the Snail"; *Shankpainter,* "The Sick Fox," "Winter Hand"; *The New England Review,* "Going Back, Not Forward, after All."

With thanks to the Fine Arts Work Center in Provincetown and the MacDowell Colony for their generous support.

For the girls of Laughing Stock Farm

CONTENTS

SUN Tongue ⋯ **11**
Eve Leaves ⋯ **12**
Going Back, Not Forward, after All ⋯ **13**
Red or Clear ⋯ **14**
His Last Story: Scratchy Landings ⋯ **16**
Father on Black Ice ⋯ **18**
Apprentice ⋯ **21**
No Thanks ⋯ **22**
The Secret Seems to Be ⋯ **23**
The Hawk ⋯ **25**
In the Country Town ⋯ **27**
Laundry ⋯ **29**
Work, Every Day ⋯ **30**
We Study Madame Curie ⋯ **31**
The Nursing Home ⋯ **32**
Dream: the Job ⋯ **33**
The Nun at Grand Central ⋯ **35**
The Sidewalk Cracked ⋯ **37**
Awake after a Year of Nights with You ⋯ **38**
The World's Refrain: "But Not Beyond" ⋯ **39**
Door ⋯ **40**

SALT Pickles ⋯ **43**
Eve's Garden ⋯ **44**
To My Sins ⋯ **47**
The Sick Fox ⋯ **48**
This Comes First ⋯ **49**
Life of a Girl ⋯ **51**
The Heart Is a Muscle ⋯ **53**
Sleep of the Snail ⋯ **54**

Winter Hand ... **55**
Emily Dickinson at Prayer ... **56**
Vertigo ... **57**
Just Once I Want to Write a Gentle Thing ... **58**
To Your Tongue ... **59**

MOON
The Function of Clouds ... **63**
Look ... **64**
What Is the Name
 of the Baby in the House? ... **65**
When You Unloose ... **66**
First Job ... **67**
Approaching the Hour ... **69**
Song for the Mother ... **70**
The Goat ... **72**
Confection ... **73**
R.S.V.P. to the Ninth
 Wedding Invitation of 1988 ... **74**
Walking down Court Street ... **75**
The Red Angel ... **77**
Hope ... **78**
Dear Dad, ... **79**
The Teacher ... **80**
The Air They Breathe ... **81**
Fireworks and the Decision ... **82**
Winter ... **83**
Blue Heron ... **84**

About the Word Works ... **86**

SUN

TONGUE

Think of something unlikely to live
in the mouth. Little rubber
rug, pincushion stippled
and pink. Old carrot, slug
lolling in the salty
mist of the Oregon coast.
There are traces of a residue
chemists refuse to analyze. Now go
to the mirror and watch
the tortoise paddling, the rope
tricks. Granny in the window,
back-alley love nest, a big
misunderstanding back at
the factory. It's the oval
office, also the diplomat
who recoils when the teeth
carve up an émigré, tactlessly
crunching the bones.

EVE LEAVES

The Lord God planted His righteous plot:
all the orange trees in rows, paths of polished
Japanese stones, a black canary at each corner. And
on the last day He created

bait. He wanted to find out what would happen
if two new beings, the perfect—perhaps the only—
examples of *tabula rasa,* were faced
with the most tempting temptation

and everything to lose. We blame
Eve, of course, because we
are she. Curious, uppity, I mean, and smart.
She saw the trap. Still, when next He paid a call,

apple cores dotted the ground. What made Him so
mad was the deliberate trail of apples
leading straight to the tree.
What no one says (though we know it)

is how it was a setup. He left them naked
and alone. He tiptoed back, saw them
glistening in the dark and delighted
from His shivering crown to His black god-shoes

when he heard her shin up, heard the snatch
of fruit from the branch, the first wet
crunch. We think Eve knew it. We're pretty sure,
for as she left the garden, we heard her slam the door.

GOING BACK, NOT FORWARD, AFTER ALL

I saw my father's catch
the light once, softly
at the hem of his shirt.
He came in with the spoon
and cough syrup. Cherry
on my lips, sticky, a hand
on my head, and sleep.

So I expected kindness and quiet:
the penis was a funny flower.
Instead? I don't dismiss the rude
introductions I could number—
gate crasher, drag racer, the dog warden,
the kind we called professor for the way
it pontificated through afternoons—but
let's look back farther and marvel: how little
boys were dying to demonstrate
that grape or nose or pod
where the cleft should have been.
Bruce Clark used to give us his lunch
if we'd look! And once we all took off our pants

and ran through the field so the feathery heads
brushed our thighs. Now when you
come to bed from the bathroom, so musically
emptied, the silver plum
dips and bobs in its bristle
of wreath full as Christmas or a welcome
tide and I think, *Now*
we're getting somewhere.

RED OR CLEAR

So the first time, he turned down the driveway,
borrowed car up to the hubs in black floodwater,
and parked where the drive ended in a bank
of branches and river hair,
carried her back to the house,
her wheelchair, and there was her favorite hen
washed in under the kitchen step,

red mop churned to a clod.
And the garden always floated off,
just patches of gravel and silt, mudgullies
wide as your boot. Old frost-bitten stumps
of pumpkin plants bent, or flattened, or gone.
And plastered here and there, bleached
packets that marked the rows last year.

And every time, he thinks he should take her away,
and if only he had the money in the bank,
and maybe someday…even if the same
sound of water rises and tolls
in his dreams and he wakes with blackness plugging
his lungs, her small hand
jogging him: wake up, wake up.

And every time, she waits until his back is turned
to cry for the hen, or the good soil scoured away
down the valley, or the bare roots of the lilac
struggling by the kitchen door. She wishes he
didn't have to carry her, floodtime or ever,
or empty her bedpan out the window,
for pain twists her less than this

wash of obligation.
Today they're "catching their breath," as she
puts it, reading the Sears catalogue. He sits
on the porchrail by her chair. They watch
the sun go and speculate will it be red or clear
and hear the river back low
in its black boulders hum.

HIS LAST STORY: SCRATCHY LANDINGS

How Bigtit Luelle got her name? Well, back
when I was jacking logs, running my mismatch
team up Woodford Mountain, I found
Delmer's gold watch on the ground and kept it for a week.
Damn fool lost it, damn fool could do without.
Do without, now there's a word Luelle don't know. One
husband warn't enough for old Bigtit. The name?
Why'd you think? One tit down to here, the other
you'd hardly notice. Men was crazy about her, straight-out
crazy, and Skunk never seemed to mind. More than once
I've seen him have a Friday beer with one of her boyfriends.
Well, I was digging a grave for Delmer,
not that he was dead, just he said I owed him a favor
or else he'd spread it around about me holding onto his watch,
so I took his turn at the churchyard. I like that.
Delmer never would've known
that I carried his timepiece in my pocket six days,
except I told him myself. He needed to know it could
have been the end of that watch.
So I'm there digging and up struts Luelle to watch me
up to my neck in that grave, and she dingle-dangles
her legs right in the hole. I'm not that kind
of crazy man, so I told her off.
I says, What you come waggling up for, Bigtit,
me to come squeeze that horn?
It just come out that way.
I didn't repeat it around, well, just told my brother, Orrin.
But in two days it was spread all over the mill.
Must have been ten years later I heard her son John Bent
say to his brother, "Bigtit wants us to dinner Sunday,"
not even a crack of a smile.

Yuh, I was a man for nicknames. Way past when I lost
the farm, they still laid the town out as
Stinkin Lincoln, Moses Row, Champagne Hill.
Down there, past the doctors' parking lot, you can see old
Roaring Fork and the graveyard growed up
in raspberries. I call it Scratchy Landings.

FATHER ON BLACK ICE

We step onto the lake, empty
platter of white.
Dark huts dot
the drifted, scalloped
vastness, huts
of the regular men.
We go way
out and dig,
leather mittens lapping
the snow. The ice below
is a black
mirror, black as
an animal's eye!
I am sure we
have found something new
that no one else
knows, not men in huts, not
Mom or my sister
home at the tiny
stove in the play-
room. He tries
to explain: "Vision
is just the eye
taking in reflected
light." What is
he talking about?
"Watch." He drills with
the auger and shavings
come up, clear and white
in the sun. Not black. My life
is heaven and hell and
I am almost
twelve and there are fish

in the dark like backwards
stars below us. Can
they breathe?
What do they
eat? What makes it
worthwhile to go
on living in
such circumstances?
Are there weeds
to brush against?
Sleek, bright, even
under the lid of shadow,
long and tapering,
maybe shifting to
ease the doubts
or kinks in their drowsing
panels of flesh for
no soothing
currents could persist under
such a hand as this
ice. Among them our lines
go down. Do they see
a hook as a shard
of light when it drops,
a way out of darkness without
edge or measure? We catch
them. They drip and
flap when we lift
them into the silver air.
Gills flare, gashed
red. The slick jewels
of their eyes. He
catches me
pouring cups of water
over them, filling
the gills to make them

live. He
knows, so
he shows me how to kill.
One thumb in the mouth,
bend the backbone till
it snaps. Feel it
go? It is cruel
what they feed us,
that we eat. "You will
not always
be so unhappy."
He promises.
I want him
to say more, want
to ask him, "Who am
I to you, now
you have pulled me
from the hole
and let me live?"

·

APPRENTICE

High on a half-clad roof, I hand Uncle Duff
another stack of sharp blue slates
which he takes with ease and
leans against his boot.

Wind latches to our sleeves and pantlegs,
even the elms, dry with disease, bend.
I carry a sheet of plywood up
to cover the hole we bored in the rotten roof

and the wind, perceiving a sail, applies itself.
If I clap my body to the ladder with all my strength,
I can just live through this.
Duff says, "Let's have that over here."

Seems like for him the slates
fall into line but my rows dip
or climb. My hammer slides over the edge, thunks
on lumber below and skitters off into nettles.

But when the schoolbus passes,
I know they can see me, home
because my help is needed in the world and at least
my nails drive straight.

I'm standing taller when it happens:
my uncle the carpenter hammers
his own thumb—"Shit!"—and sticks it in his mouth
like any other man or girl.

NO THANKS

There are fathers who are worse than fathers.
Take Jane's: one day he took sleeping
pills, but she found him. After the stomach pump
he talked about innocence all the time.
He wore the word like a new skin.
He wrote letters about the light an orchard gives off,
about how he is—we all are—Christ. Jane,
who made him live that day by dialing
911 and stating clear and slow
the proper address and means of poison, Jane will
read the stories when she grows up, all about
her step-father's new silvery eyes, how he has risen
and the halo of Christ is everywhere he looks. He says

he wants to sing to us. He spreads his shoulders wide.
I know Jane, or I did when she was small, but
I know. How her first dad drinks and wishes
she were his to care for, to give in to mildly. Now,
this second father's telling of his
lovely suffering and how fireflies
ignite the trees behind his house.

But it's her house too. So go away, mister,
we're all lonely here. She'll see it soon enough.
Christ! She'll come down to breakfast thirteen years old
and see in your eyes: herself, already thirty-one
or fifty… I hope the pulse pinches
at your wrists and your lungs wheeze
for every breath. I have no patience left. Do you
plan to take her on your
shoulders? When she rests her palm
on your bald spot, your pain will be small compared
to hers, will pucker, throb, and veer away. Whose
innocence then, whose shoulders?

THE SECRET SEEMS TO BE

Every year at the edge of the wood
my father leans his rifle
on the fence, calls the steer
to the rail.

Yesterday Frank said, "Do you want help
with the slaughter?" My father
cleared his throat, looked up
through the beech.
The reaping wind had left them
half their gold. Gray boles
rose straight as smoke on a cold day.
He's always liked this plainness.
He thumbed his beard
and said, "No need. I'm able.
Don't come unless you want to."

I've never watched, or offered,
but once I dreamed the black hulk
hung by the heels and steaming
on the chill fall day.

The red, the black, he fed each steer,
filled the rattling rick and even
went along with giant
games of tag. His jacket flapped as
Dad and steer dodged each other's lunges,
spun, braced, stiff-kneed. Jets
of breath blotted the open air. Or I'd look
out and see Dad leaning, cigarette lit,
against the companionable bulk.

And he's found a way
to do this.
The secret seems to be
solitude, speed, efficiency.

I took Frank out walking
where goldenrod bucked and bent.
We leaned against the wind, which brought us
one report. Milkweed rattled
against our legs, and through thick, dull boots
I felt the grass press
to the ground, spring, give a lift
to every step, even the driest wisp
possessing a life of its own.

THE HAWK

The summer Schuyler died—Dad's
friend "Sky"—and his mother
found him where he fired the shot
in his old room, we were raising
the hawk on raw meat
and watching his wings grow. Gram
started with hamburg on the end of a toothpick
and it ate, unknowing of our desire

that it live. Dad wasn't sure it could,
but Gram was always taking in
difficult birds. In its cage it molted the ugly fluff
and grew. Then we knew what to call him, since the red
color of the feathers of the tail
was male. He stood on the screened porch with eyes
half-hooded, beak ajar, as if panting. He glared.
Sometimes I hardly dared watch as he gulped

the pulpy meat. Soon she had to leave his meals
on the china plate and you could hear the beak
snap snap as it snatched the shreds and clots of flesh.
I watched the talons wince. Glance
like a razor too as the foot that meant food
crossed the doorstep. He rocked
from side to side, waiting for the plate to touch
the floor, then dove down in a wind of hunger

on the new big wings. I turned thirteen.
Nothing stopped me from watching.
One day in spring she took him out—he'd been inside
a fall and a winter—and lifted him up on a garden glove.
He stared around him for a long white breath, then shot

up in a heave of wings, her hand dropping back hard.
Then, as she tells the story, he swore at her, one furious shriek
for having kept him in, and flew away in a straight line.

He didn't come back. Dad thinks that's him
with a mate living up the back hill. We watch them
coasting on sheets of air, carried in spirals that boom
and gyre to the sun even on the coldest days when their screams
are hungry and the fields below are bare.
Dad listens to them early, splitting wood
or after milking. His head tilts like Gram's as the keening
flames overhead, a cold blue burn.

IN THE COUNTRY TOWN

I want that no farmers go to the bank,
no cows founder here,
no fields blight, and no crops
molder in the shed.

No barns lean,
and creak, and fold.
No hills grown over in sumac
and sickly elm.

Children won't drift through the school or
forget their five lines of Frost.
In the flat tin townhall no men and women
vote in the latest taxbill.

No new prostitutes, just the one who knits
by the payphone. No new pharmacist,
please; the same one and his shaky hands
—they don't go wrong—and his blue

minted breath. The same A & P, iceberg
lettuce and eggs so translucent
nobody buys. We'll drive up the road
for brown eggs from Svitag, the same Swede.

The same corner for asking directions,
same women on errands to point the strangers
straight, the same bare blink
of engagement rings, same small but

authentic stones. I want to buy my wine
at the Santerres' place, always, and this time
I'll get no farther on the road out of town
than Metzgers' field of fresh-cut hay.

The farm inspector in her Oldsmobile,
testing the county's teats for TB, stops
to talk dairy with the Reynolds Bros.,
the same every season,

and dawdling in the orchard until dark,
she, too, wishes she could stay,
the way the sky can stay one
cold cup of stars, immovable stars.

LAUNDRY

Medieval sacks bulge through the door
of the corner laundromat where trash moving south
sweeps the street of leaves and the dust
that blows in from upstate.
In the rumble and fall

of driers, things shrink. A woman swings the porthole
open, fights back the twisted cloth,
and feels. Still too damp. Another
quarter. Spin fast and hotter and small.
At the counter, whole families fold up

the week's clean wear: sleeve to sleeve
smoothed, stray socks brought to heel
and rolled into fists, jeans bent into mats,
one pale Sunday blouse to hang. We go round
and round and start over, whiteness and trouble.

WORK, EVERY DAY

"And so I have to,
I have to. So you
can live here for free,
you fucking lazy bum. I have
to, so you can live here for free, you nothing,
and eat my fucking eggs
for your lunch. I have to."

(After cleaning Mr. Hoagland's, five dollars
an hour, she finds her son still flat
on his back, it's Friday, and he's
playing electric keyboards in bed. Funk
makes the paintings—Mary, mother
of Jesus, rolling her eyes, and the wedding pose
done from a color photograph—thump on the wall.
Six o'clock Saint Anthony's bells drown him
out, leave her voice scouring the kitchen.

Night. And her highbush roses,
big as red balloons and as easy on the air,
spread syrup in the dark. They're throated
with heat, sweet as bread.)

She shrieks, "My eggs! My eggs!"
The son's light snaps on
into the rose-thick garden
where nobody goes.

WE STUDY MADAME CURIE

We see her at the counter steady as a log,
the flame
stemming from her fingers
into the metal mouth of the burner
to which she bends. She manages the cord
and panels of her apparatus. The gas tongue laps,
an opal, at her hand. Why isn't she
worried? And where's her pride? Look at that stain
on her cuff. Whatever she's looking for, we
do not understand, but it's not right
to see her white sleeves gleam, to brace
as if we are the thin-walled crystal,
to feel her manly grip upon the glass.

THE NURSING HOME

Seems everyone's quitting and last
night she spoke pleasantly to only two
on her ward.
              "Hard to remember
that they ask you a thing six times
because they can't remember they've asked
six times before."
                She goes every night
and turns them and cleans them and listens.
"Oh," says Martha, lying in pee, "That Marie
smell like shit!" Joanna asks,
                          What is the good
of going to church? What is the good of washing
my hair?" But she goes. Turns them.
And spoons in the food.
                  Comes home.
Has her small bourbon. Goes to bed
and dreams of a house where there's room
for everyone to live. And everyone
                          comes home.
She wakes to the hungry scratch at the back door
of the big white dog and the small black dog
and goes down and lets them in.

DREAM: THE JOB

1.
Mornings, I approach: a tall white house.
The paint peels in scrolls that rustle
and flap. Door's bolted. Go around, get
ladder and buckets, lift the runny brush, begin.

2.
Some days I wear my job like a head
of redhot curlers. On my shoulders it's a doghouse
full of angels, saintly salesmen
selling each other: long-stemmed roses wrapped
in cellophane, toxic waste in barrels,
keen cups of lemonade.

3.
The cyclone circus: at a canter, tasks circle
me, woman with whip. A pink feather
between each black pair of ears. Don't trust
them, keep the ring of hooves
prodding on. Fetlock-deep in sawdust,
they push toward five o'clock.

4.
Finally, something flies: maybe like
monarchs swarming, a drift of monarchs
that twists through layers of weeds and up.
My hands feel clean, my feet are still.

5.
Why not just say this person works
and gets paid and it passes the day? But I see
the coffee pot like an old stump on the stove
and remember: nothing is just
what it is, not for long. Not for now.

THE NUN AT GRAND CENTRAL

Subway uptown to make the train
to Albany my mother my father who
I've noticed might be dying and I can't
believe where this lady just put her
elbow. Doors open doors
close people pack all
the space with flesh some have
too much some too little and then
they get off. I timed it
too close run up
the first stairs a yellow
so bright you'll take note
not trip crack your skull thus
inconveniencing many busy
citizens who like you like me must
catch that train it's life
or death! Since I'm still young
I leap up stairs and save
fifteen seconds maybe more one arm out
stretched I rush the door
that whines out clangs
back and now the brass rail
where all New Yorkers drop a deadly
germ or two a skim of finger/
palm prints sliding down
or up. I heave skip every
other step but huff half
way deeply regret my heavy
boots that knock and clamber five
last satanic steps and there she
sits. The blue glaze of cataracts
garnishes her dark bulk plus
a white paring from temple

to temple. She's as soft
and white as a cellar toad.
I cannot give though
there's always change in my hand
when I meet the one-armed bum
on Atlantic Avenue and the mad
Lebanese who shines my stoop
with his jacket at night. Only
two coins in her flat
basket no one stops and she goes
on sitting six years now of trips
north and she has not missed
one appointment nor I. I'm going home
with just enough to pay my fare
through the tunnel rocking as lights
like eyes above us flicker. Everyone's
young and thin on this train small wallets
of work in hand we stake out single
seats and head home in duty love
and faith. We don't bear
children don't plough fields clear
canals or push like pilgrims
to the west. The gold day fades
we cross the marshes wild
ducks flush from the reeds
and water at the clatter of wheels
on rail. The lights steady
point at our faces and laps
circles we wait to fill.

THE SIDEWALK CRACKED

The smooth new slab grew
a black fracture that fattened until
the jagged halves were free. One rose
a little. One sank. Pedestrians
began to snag a pointed toe or heel
and almost land, praying, in the grass.
Our own children skinned their knees again and again.
The crack bloomed feathery weeds. First,
we pulled them up,
then we mowed them down,
then we just let it go.

AWAKE AFTER A YEAR OF NIGHTS
WITH YOU

The rooster started his matins
full of bark and milk, and blinking
his blank and fishy eye at the rim of the world,
he fumbled for the first note

that wobbled up and pinned itself above the rusty
trough of light just beginning
to spill as the smells—

cabbage under frost, barn muck, moldy
chrysanthemum—rose toward the summer's last swallows
diving for bugs. It seemed, standing with you
as I've become accustomed to do, that everything

was his when he uncorked for it the lusty
unprecedented yowl.
It snagged us to the window, remember, and we
admired how he stretched on his thick yellow toes, how then
he could bend his head, simply, to peck in the dirt for seed.

THE WORLD'S REFRAIN: "BUT NOT BEYOND"

You may have this one dollar.
You may measure this favor.
You may calculate the world's appetite for snow.
You may go to school and be ruled.

Now you may walk with yesterday's feet.
Now you may take one deep breath.
Now you may weave your hair into a noose.
Now you may love someone else's child.

And soon you may light the blue wick.
And soon you may mount desire.
And soon you may drive home.

DOOR

An
egg ticks, black cricket
fiddling in the grave: unmother.
(Other women say I desire this.)

But I never asked or permitted,
locked the porch door every night,
and the front. But you're here, cousin

jot, latchkey, muzzle, seahorse, little friend, you
are the single dangerous thing. (They
give their lives for you, they give you
their lives.)

SALT

PICKLES

                        The day God put up the first batch
of green tomato pickles,
              bobbing in their buckets
of brine, he knew
        what he was doing
                     on Delancy Street.
Adam he ordered
        to distribute names
                and trouble,
but to those humbler
        denizens
            he merely said,
"Go forth and soak."
        So they drink in
                the sweet salt
and glow like traffic lights
        in the curbside
                  murk
of Murray's pickle stand.
        They shame the dills,
half-dills and peppers.
        The bin never empties. To live forever,
you must go there every
        day, eat two,
                or more, eat four.
Float, friends! I taste you
        and am glad.
And now I'm not sure
        the green word GOD didn't roll
from the first brain
        when a bright
                burst of Eve-early salt
astounded the first tongue.

EVE'S GARDEN

So on he fares, and to the border comes
Of Eden, where delicious Paradise,
Now nearer, crowns with her enclosure green,
As with a rural mound the champain head
Of a steep wilderness, whose hairy sides
With thicket overgrown, grotesque and wild,
Access denied...
                    Paradise Lost (IV 132-137)

1. Vulva

How like a coconut: cuppable,
shaggy, and milky-sweet
within. A soft sly sneaker, or
it's a big baby buggy! On fat
silver springs it rolls
through the sun. This is the hairy hill
where Milton's Eve reclines, resting
as if on a jelly
donut, white sugar powdering
her thighs, and she sighs, she rocks
and rises on her powder puff.

2. Clitoris

This pheasant's heart
beats in its feathered nest.
Lucifer's face alight between black
burlap wings, glossy and salt
as an olive. The whetstone
her hands return to. Oh, ship's
biscuit! The roan bronc who's already bucking
in the chute. Pineapple:
its tart cantankerous meat.

3. Labia minora

Down the center, little rooster wattles,
pressed like moist hands palm to palm,
these elephant ears hide-tough but
delicate as sea-monkeys that came
dry and dead in the mail
but—JUST ADD WATER!—squirmed
to life under the lens. Pink tippling
chimneys, iris edges plump as snails
dizzy in their shells. They're like some lace
of the sea, sheltered and spongy as chanterelles.

4. Hymen

The imploded bugle,
Hard not to believe these nubs aren't cancerous
growth, random, protuberant.
Remember the gleam of the gate, the keeping out and in.

5. Vagina

Rippled as stairs worn
slick by the feet of nuns, century
after century, their words still
susurrant in the passage.
They rocked on their knees, mopping this
floor, under the rose window the
sponges appearing soaked with blood.
At chapel they kissed in the dark
their palms and fingers, felt themselves
grow wet at the salty crease
where the elbow bends.

6. Cervix

Old fish-lips, complacent
as a potato. Satin pillow passive
but for the final involuntary gasps at
the always-unexpected capitulation to pleasure.
At the head of the throneroom, she
shudders and there's the power
behind the queen: the egg
wades slowly to pasture, to rupture
and rapture, to translucent blooded anchorage, and exit.

7. Womb

Exit: to dream vulvas, and of Eve's
expulsion where lush trees rocked,
tipped with pink fruit, and of the dew sinking
its icy silver tongues into the grass. Exit:
to dream the round fountain
at the center whose reflection casts
our own faces back, saying,
this is all, this miraculous kite
that pulls you—back—we can almost touch—
back to the wet egg wavering,
to the moment when the seed
burst toward us, began to climb, the slide and
jostle to be the one, the first succulent
hello, the savior and the brand.

TO MY SINS

As an infant, I cranked out sounds.
I found I loved to lie.
Soon I wanted a lover from the circus
with four hands or more. In my sleep
I fucked very fat women on a bridge.

(My heart was a toad for a while:
sometimes a week passed and still
the ground and sky weren't themselves.
You know, go for a walk and nothing
happens, nothing feels.)

Silence. The ease of hate.
And maybe the times I pushed
other people's children on the swings
higher than I dared to go.

THE SICK FOX

To get away I used to climb up
to the ledge in the young and overcrowded
pine. There was a bed of moss, pungent, moist.
I used to imagine someone, bringing him
there to... I hardly knew what.

Then one dream curdled real:
the first He and I went past
buttons in that green bed. The metallic
swag of his braces-flavored kisses,
the sour smell of our pubic hair, matted
by jeans, the hike, heat, keeping our eyes
closed, shame as alive
as the penis wincing between us.

For instance, we never came:
I think he felt it would be impolite.
And who knew how? One day, alone,
I surprised from the bed
of moss a fox—but
it staggered away so unwildly, ratty tail dragging.
No magnificent red brush, just a damp
rag. Crazy kid—I went home and asked my parents
what could we do.

"And even if it gets better, it will just come
after the hens," Mom said.
"It's sad, I know," said Dad, "but
let it go." Not the fire
animal seen once as I stood
by the barn, looking where Dad pointed to the crown
of the hill. But a sad, flattened creature,
crawling almost, slow and self-effacing, cowering away.

THIS COMES FIRST

> *for Julie Holter, 1943-1981,*
> *paralyzed below the shoulders, July 1963*

I admired and needed you not
because you suffered, but because
when I brushed your hair,
you'd say, "Harder, harder!"
and lean into the bristles,
let the sun's hand
cup the back of your neck.

Was it the most you could feel?
It was all I could do for you,
and believe me, it was hard enough
for me in my black turtleneck,
hiding in three years of adolescent fat,

to hold the handle tighter,
plunge the head of the brush
deep in your thicket of hair
and push as hard as you asked
against the white scalp,
to put the brush down and with my own
fingers press the skin in circles
against the bone and hear you moan
and worse, grunt, low,
to keep crawling across your skull,
even when my fingertips went numb,
even when the sounds from you stopped.

(No wonder when you told me to invite John,
I made love to him years
too early. I guess you heard through the wall.
You lay in bed all morning, didn't wake me

to empty the overnight jug of pee drained
from the bag of your body or slice the bread.
Just watched the shade flutter on the wall
until we woke.)

Life can be too soft and you
showed how to ask for it, the heat, its kind
and frightening hand:
harder, harder, more.

LIFE OF A GIRL

She won the bloody birth and her mother
sliding past in a scream. She won milk from aching
breasts, love's merciless
gum and nip, the tyranny of the soft
brown button. She won the occasional touch
for her insatiable skin and the air
in which to puke and pee. She won
sleep's soft black socket.
She won day after day right out of the grudging sky
and first furious steps across
the room, father's hand to dangle on
from sink to stove. She won her run
right down to the mailbox hanging empty.
Hard things to chew, blades
to hold. She won her mother's no,

her father's yes, a cup to fill and pour.
She won a dress that showed her legs and shoes
for other girls to envy. She won eyes
upon her, a careful slowness when men
came to see her father's cabinet.
At school a silence against the army
of dangers, the eyes along her hem.
She won the moment where she began
to think, to close
the funnels and pipes leading to that lamp,
her body, and also clothes
like black sacks in which to store the prize.
She won a Greyhound trip alone, three hours
to tell her life so far to the interested woman
on her left and, when they stopped,

a sliver of dry and salty cheese.
She won in secret
things nobody ever named,
claimed the red beat, and that heavy spongy hill,
and the tunnel she'd once descended. She won
back her veins pounding at the pinpoint
center of the world, congratulated and
exacted herself, finger by finger. So, she won
quiet. And she won through to not
winning. To Eve sucking on a nectarine. And a pot
in which to cook strong soup, and leaves, furled and fallen,
the road going home in the half-light. She won
the whole mapless mountain and the churn of tart regret
just starting to curdle, already
gathering to yellow, to clean.

THE HEART IS A MUSCLE

Big as a knee socket,
this mare-muzzle, jittery as the
kitchen timer, it mambas the blue
volts through my body. Next door, yours
does the same. These better brains
live behind our lungs. They crouch like beasts or
children and mine dips a finger into the stream
to see if it's bitter or plum.
                                      And we stumble,
occasionally careless with fuses and fire-
hazards, like that pile of rash things
we said last week over pancakes.
                                          Remember
the day we brought our hearts to this
flat mattress to fatten? They stretch to house
more mistakes than before, and now the child
can wave her arms. They graze
together steady on our black-pearled sleep
when we're gone, heavy and bright
in the dark as miners' lamps.

SLEEP OF THE SNAIL

The snail sleeps
in that doorknob of the sea,
spiral of silence with no top

or bottom. No unconscious
bubbles up, washing
through its salty thoughts,

bringing the flotsam of fear to the surface.
They even breed in their sleep,
without worrying, is this right,

is this love? Merging like Pacific currents,
parting like curtains of underwater vine.
They have no veins. They stew

in their shells like small wine-soaked
sponges, loll in the cup
of carapace. The snail sleeps

because it doesn't know it is
asleep. Crawling down its silver rope,
it dozes, rolled like the tongue

with nothing to say, curled
like a finger, the gesture
come here, perfect and crude.

Back then, their maker
didn't know what he was doing.
He just practiced

hatching headbones and light.
This is where, before artifice,
he learned.

WINTER HAND

Fish are sleeping, long and sleek
under the ice. Blank eyes lidded
in the winter dark. A fin fans,
slowly, in a dream about upriver
travel, occasional tail-twitch. Reach
your hands into the water,
slide over them, their fat flanks.

Let the heat of your hands penetrate,
let the fish feel your landlubber's touch
as you fathom your own fear of the water,
everything in it, of the ease of their sleep,
the trust or ignorance with which they hang
suspended under ice three solid months of the year.

Let your palms hover millimeters from the dorsals,
feel the brushing… Now you can touch the hard
mouths, moving identically whether they breathe
or eat or fight. Trace the frightening softness
of the bellies, and feel yourself begin to cry
the tears that have waited for you, tears
like trout finally finding the current of the river.

EMILY DICKINSON AT PRAYER

Scissored by corsets, she waited for the yeasty
dough to bake, pressed her thighs
together as heat
rippled against the panes. Look! Someone's
mind unrolled across the floor. She reeled it up
again, fingers fast from sorting green
pods and buttons. Then a fly
rumbled in her
ear, the stove
loomed blacker—her dimpled gasp filled
the kitchen. Later, upstairs, she wrote.
The attic squeezed. She winced when the syllable
GOD swelled around her heart, but, serious
as a wife, she asked for it all: the gun, dram,
pearl, ants, and God's hot hand inside her skull.

VERTIGO

This can't be random, how fields of you lean
forward, planks shy back, turns
surge from far to near, slope,
and this plane, satin as the handle
of your grandmother's fish knife! The scar,
fossil. Boulder. Shanks that furl a tent.
You're sculpted—heavy brown breakfast roll,
horizon of Iowa, butter-gold snails on a plate,
the cup of a hand making
hamburgers, pink and fat, or catching a white moth
out the window—you are all this, just to look at,
and I'm dizzy from unraveling back
and forth on the visual
rigging I've built all over,
one millimeter from your body.

JUST ONCE I WANT TO WRITE A GENTLE THING

I'll tell you a story, then,
of how as I was walking, I smelled something sugary,
elusive, spicy, you could call it,
and smoky in a sad sort of way. Also
like blossom barely born, pale and half-undone
to the wind that still might even be carrying snow,
this scent I decided to follow.
Sometimes I stumbled on the path, silver
with stones worn smooth as kindness,
or had to stop and rest among pines
where the smell settled a little, at home
with their religious and sensuous twang. Other times,
I moved fast, snatching at its mulchy sweet threads
through the air, the leaf and rotten-meat ribbons of scent,
rough tongues of tigers who have recently feasted, the living decay
of happiness, and saddle soap, the lemon urgency of sex,
honey of the air—where did it come from?
I rose panting up the slope, muscles strung on the searching
bow of my body, raised the back of my hand
to wipe away the sweat
salting my lips
and realized the smell—
the smell is me.

TO YOUR TONGUE

When you undo me in this
particular way with your tongue,
you are singing my secret name delicious
into the fat twisting petals of flesh.
Mouth to mouth we're a strange fish,
as pure as the water it swims in.

Now you glide your hands up to my
say it
beloved breasts
and linger along my   say it
irradiating waist
and around to hold and hold the
say it! say it!
irresistible hips
or rest your face for a second deep in my thigh.
I cannot believe how I have come to love this
palace, body of plain old cushion and gristle,
aging already in squiggles and puckers,
each one an ornament
where once the smooth paleness of shame.
My body glorious like a bomb.
The starfish behind my eyes.
The clouds my legs are bolted from.
Stop-lights going green in the pit of my belly.

You, tongue! Spider-racing, buffalo-stampede-
on-the-hot-yellow-plains tongue! Like the hawk
we raised, tearing tenderly into its hamburg, or
the canary riffling powder-light feathers
with its beak as fine as a fingernail. Tongue!
I want to lend you to all my friends. You have no rules,

rock and plunge on the runners of your will and drift
like a mollusk through the salt where you're glad
to live. I push myself to you as you praise
and praise and praise the body I came back to.

MOON

THE FUNCTION OF CLOUDS

We beat our silver pans
to chase the horse
back to the woods.
Our good white horse—
we never fed her,
or praised her,
or rode her,
white as the round moon,
this old—ancient—
one. Why, mother moon, do we chase
her away?

        Because, foolish,
no oats in the bin,
no oats in the bin, no oats.

At the center of the woods now
the horse is drinking.
Clouds skate across the pond.
Tamarack needles gallop down and drum
like rain or the light into our heads when we cannot stand
the beauty any more and beat
our pans, beat our pans!

LOOK

for G.G.

The breasts of old women do not speak to us.
We avoid them with our eyes.
Once we wanted just to rest
here and feel against our cheek

how plentiful the velvet food.
Our fat hands uncurled.
Sometimes, we just played the nipple
along our gums, waiting to see what would happen.

The breasts of old women
are long, or furrowed, or collapsed to soft patties,
nipples raised like Braille above the throbbing
of age. We would have to read this map

by touch to retrieve the years we dropped,
laced with ache. The women regard
them without fear. Why do we?
We do. We look away.

WHAT IS THE NAME OF THE BABY IN THE HOUSE?

What is the name of the baby in the house?
Do you see the hands opening like flowers?
Do you see something in the empty-full eyes?
Why are the legs pretending now to run?
What book will this sound someday become?
Where will a moth such as this fly away to?
Where is the father, what is his name?
How many pounds of pain in a house?
Has the mother a name?
How many are the rooms of rage?
Is compression of air around the baby the answer?
Is sweet candy for the baby an answer?
Will the bed please rise on its legs to swallow the baby?
Is there a song to save the baby?
Can the name of this baby be heard anywhere in this house?
Does the baby know yet how to count?
Does the baby know yet how to forget?
Will there be a better sound in the morning?
Are the mother's hands made of paper?
Is the father's soft voice a black window?
Is the baby's belly full of food?
Are we left in the tunnel in darkness?
Does anyone know the baby's name?

WHEN YOU UNLOOSE

This is when you unloose
what you know
    she hit me
    she hit me
This day opens and its flowers like winter breaths lift
as they open wider, into leopard paws, into baskets of snow.
The sleeping world loosely rocks
on its hinge. Your hand drifts open and shut.
Rise up on the breath of the world! Dull keys
fall behind, below. The meanings of the word KEY,
the word HAND are gone. Burnt. You are the puff
of ash that's left, no, a petal
bathing the air with your passage,
bathing yourself against the bright air.

FIRST JOB

The other girl's name was Sheila
and we washed tables in the lunchroom.
She had short black hair curly
all over her head. Her nose was a wavy line,
uncertain. She was tall, gangly, but I noticed
her hips swelling out, the bony curve. We were friends
for this twenty minutes every day. In the cafeteria
the women big and rounded as tomatoes, bulky
in their print dresses, made extra money for the farm
with this morning job—serving us stewed prunes
and ravioli, bite-size foods. They moved as solid
and otherworldly as horses. Women who'd
given birth, who cooked for hundreds, women
who carried whole farms in their minds, season after season
the knowing of what comes next and what needs doing,
and kransekake baked for everyone by Saturday.
They know the number of lambs and the hours of the men.

The women silent and big behind counters handed us
gray rags in old tomato juice cans of hot water and a squirt
of detergent, and we worked down the long tables,
talking. I liked how our swirly smears
overlapped in the middle. One day I joked
about Richard and Linda, kissing. She said,
"I've done that. My grandfather makes me."
I began, "So what? Everyone's—" but she stood back,
funny, twisting her rag. Her eyes dark
and blank as the sick calf's at home. "What?" I said,

"What?" She told how for two years he's been taking
off her shirt, how he rubbed his face there—
"Even before I had these," she said, pointing
to the breasts that nosed into her untucked blouse—

how at Christmas he pulled down her pants and put his thing
inside her, "there," how he does this every week now,
while the women cook. "Does it hurt?" I said.
"At first. Now it's… nothing." Around us the slick
tables gleamed. The water cans breathed steam. Ten
years old, what did we understand?
"I can't wait till they catch him," she said.
"Why don't you just stop?"
"They make me go in there when they cook. It's *Sunday*,"
and she looked at me. She seemed tall,
so tall and far away.

I felt sick when I got home, and went to bed.
Why didn't I tell? My mother's hand on my cheek.
Why didn't I? My gentle father in the door.
"Hey, feel any better?" I could have told him.
I could have. He would have listened.
It never occurred to me.

APPROACHING THE HOUR

Because I left the cream on the table
Because instead I chose the red pants
Because she could not explain me to the crowd

Because she never kept back a slice for herself
Because she still dreamed my lips tugging her nipple
Because I am her tendril

Because I knew all the roads away
And I couldn't help the blood between my legs
Because her mother crumbled and died

Because she did not appear on my canvas
Because the snake said *darling, darling*
And I am her root

Because I built a galloping fire
And whittled in secret with a big sharp knife
And she picked glass from my scalp with tweezers

Because between us the king's crown of razors
And under us the musical tipsy planet
And love is old, old

Because this letter is not for her
Because she reaches for the plain loaf
And everything's a question now

And the bicycle rusted all winter
Because making me better was a hunger
Because pain swerves to every house

Because nothing's left on the plate
And now she must stand alone

SONG FOR THE MOTHER

I want the air to lift you
I want the air to carry

The air will lift
The air will carry you

It will open the fists of lilac for you
It will roll the sun
Down the hill into the dim hollow
Where your father built the house

It will string stars for you in loops
That brush the top of Woodford Mountain
It will sing too and
Bring bread
Will open the door for leaves
To sweep the cold kitchen
Will lift and carry   It will
Open the veins in your
Mother's hands and legs   loosen
Her corroded joints and for the first time
In years she will stand   will
Take one step   another   she will
Be tall   out of her wheelchair for the first
Time since you were five
You will not have to help her
She will come out tall through the door
That the air has opened for free
Just for the pleasure of a door standing open

I see you too
Sitting in a chair
Face closed as the earth though you can walk if you choose

And the air is not moving around us
Have an apple
Take a big green one tart
And hard   enjoy the juice   do not share
Please take an apple

And the air will shine the moon for you
It will bring the river down forgiving at floodtime
The white chickens will flop free
From the little house where you were sent
With an axe
The air will fill the school with books
For you
Will soften your father's hand
It will join your name with blackbirds
Warm your mother's saintly smile
Will oil your name like a pearl
Roll it like a crown
The honey air will promise
This name is good
This name is beautiful
All this beauty is true
Is for you   you   to graze upon

THE GOAT

Funny, talking to a goat.
She seized the grass in her teeth,
ate gallantly, dallying, and listened.

What a squall in my brain as we talked
of sisterhood. Once the goat commented
on my mildness with scorn.

Have a voice, she said, you're not some virgin
looking for sentiment any longer;
look for something big, like solitude.

Past this goat ran the singing
stream, full of the eggs of fish,
full of the quarrels of life.

CONFECTION

I think the great poets when they write
about love are remembering one-night stands
that perch their post-facto
perfection on the tips
of those fantastical tongues.

A tongue can go on for years,
believing that if it reaches, reaches,
it will finally track down that one taste
somewhere between salt and rose, between
fur and wet cardboard, between saddles

and verbena, then fall on its moist face
in the stableyard of passion,
so quickly met and matched
that the brain, old Puritan, faints.
Those poets, what do they think they'll find?

Imagination lags behind, panting, and only the tongue,
the wet, salty, salted, squirming, pink, pinker, blazing
tongue remembers anything at all about that night,
the one the poets write about,
sighing, Oh, that was love.

R.S.V.P. TO THE NINTH WEDDING OF 1988

At the ninth wedding I will not
greet each delighted aunt and chat
with blow-dried cousins interested in computerized
airport scrutiny. Nor will I file with strangers relying
on politeness across the fading lawn
and wait for someone I know
to slip between two urns of white petunias
and join her parents, father clenching
and unclenching his left hand, mother's heels
sticking awkward in the grass.

I will not hear her dyed-to-match tread approach
the man in black, say the words I cannot believe
anyone alive understands. I will not see
another ring climb down another finger. I will not pose
another toast with bubbles that have fizzed away
before each guest has got a glass, nor dip
with two fingers for the coy strawberry there,
nor accept cheese from a toothpick colored pink,
nor crowd around to see dry cake bisected
by the pair sharing their first knife. Yes, this

is my warning, old friends, good people.
As the caterer flicks tiny slices
onto a hundred paper plates, I will not
seek you out and kiss you as the mosquitoes swarm
in on groom and bride. I do not propose
to know the answers. But to the ninth wedding I will not go.

WALKING DOWN COURT STREET

By Caputo's Bakery there's a waft
of almond left, an edge of cardamon.
The mimosa dusts down
yellow onto the green four-door.
Leaning, a woman, her shadow
like a spoon to stir the air,
tastes a man.
The engine's running.

It's a long walk home,
tiring, but I can't sleep—
the upstairs neighbors fight.
"You think I'm a bum, so
I should sleep in the street?"
Every night I hear them,
every morning I smell
their bacon cure in the pan.

I helped at my friend May's
wedding. We drove to the church together.
She swore, "There's something wrong
with the brakes." I know about cars,
as much as the next woman. Those brakes
were fine. I fixed my eye
on an apple tree in the distance,
kept my mouth shut. Hard to say
what no one wants to hear.
Flower arrangements
sagged in the back seat. We inched
toward her altar, May dabbing
at the brakes. Still,

she married him.
Today I walk home
to a man who took a long time
to make up his mind, like a bed.
And there they are, the car
tunes to them as it runs. Another
pint of petals falls. Maybe it's goodbye,
maybe it's a bridal car.

THE RED ANGEL

The Red Angel is assigned to live in my house for one year.
I give her the good guest room and
bring her tiny crabs and cherries for breakfast,
but she bounds from bed to jerk the curtains open.

She has a way of dressing and undressing.
Her breath fries the dahlias in the yard.
The Red Angel wants to kiss me with her cactus tongue.
She wants to bite the fat calves of the baby.

The Red Angel twists knobs off the stereo,
the heads off dolls. She knows how to make
a whole life into a word with a single meaning.
She finds my unsent letters and reads them

at dinner to the crowd. When she sleeps, her wings
are leafy, limp, breathing. This angel gleams
a more dangerous red every day, every hour
hotter. Each minute quivers like a pin. It would be easy

to run away, but without her I am weak… Always I'd choose
the Red Angel rather than live without this
knowing how hot and heavenly
our sin, this angel I took into my house to live.

HOPE

like a stern pagoda
a wind rising
the gate broken

for your mother's survival
hearts are only tissue and gristle
sniffing like a mutt in the alley

nudges at your earlobe seductive
jugular pumping with fever
this madman sits down beside me

my murderous intentions continue
the hollow you reserve is for me
uncanny faith of this child is for me

white as imagined bones
grills its trout on the embers of houses
licking its wounds and licking its wounds

grab the pie cutter! the milk glass! the table is trembling!
one trolley uphill creaking
you match my lips exactly

we used to believe in god
green as bottles chard rain
under a manhole cover so lift! lift!

like the abacus clacking
when the milk came we were not surprised no never
we did not bite the nipples we never

manifesto of black
dredging Tuesday for light on the river
spark in the heavens satellite or star

www.ingramcontent.com/pod-product-compliance
Lightning Source LLC
Chambersburg PA
CBHW031207090426
42736CB00009B/811

DEAR DAD,

Do the corn stalks still clatter
in the back field? Always spooked me—
you know, is someone there?
Once in the spruce in that hedgerow

I found a rabbit hung in a noose.
It fell bone by bone
as the flesh raveled,
as the cartilage shrank.

The rope swung there for years,
frayed. I still wonder
who did this. Evil boys,
farmer with a reason?

Take care of yourself.
Enjoy the air, this moon
climbing your fence, the elm and sky.
Sometimes I wonder that I left, and why.

THE TEACHER

for Jane Cooper & Grace Paley

In her office one Thursday,
she heard the chainsaw kick in,
ran to stand between two men
and the magnolia. And she wouldn't budge.
The tree stands.

In April from her office window she watches
the white flowers thick across the crown
and on the lower branches,
in the hemlock shade,
sparse and upright as candles.

But now she can't retire, sure they'll
cut it when she's gone. In a high wind
it rubs against the eave. They say
it could bend the foundation, make it buckle
as roots fatten and lift.

Today two students pass her window.
One says, "Death, death, death,
that's all anyone talks about any more,"
and flicks some ash into the grass.
What if she left, just left?

She wants to walk straight
across the field, half-choked with early hay,
and mount the hill where one pear tree
has gone unpruned and unsung for as long
as she remembers but has always bloomed.

THE AIR THEY BREATHE

I say she is a nice girl. I say
she is bad. She's a hero
but she's yellow to the core. She
is black rain at Christmas. The cow's
green dream. This girl is mute and
she won't stop talking.

I say the newspaper blows rat-backward
up the street, past her feet.
I say dogs love
the girl. I say they take her away
limb by limb.
I say she huddles among other girls. I say

she blazes. I say the girls hate the air
any of them breathes. I say they're in love
with each other. I say to you I'm heavy help,
all I can do is watch them take the rope
in their hands, and dance, yes, slam
their heels against the land.

FIREWORKS AND THE DECISION

Fenced by flares that spear the star-stamped
sky, I lift my friend's baby, brace
against his trembling. His cries are half
joy, half terror as the sparks
bite and coil and seem to alight
in the grass around us. He stares, clasps,
may carry this burial of light into the years.

Home, my own white tree is dropping
leaves like knives. They clatter
on the stones. Sometimes singing
makes it worse, this walk in the woods.
The wind! The wind's pushing us indoors
but I want horns and hooves and a
cannon for a heart.

In our bed, a curve. A life
of its own, antennae, frail
and tasting how delicate we are. We hear
rain coming, up the walk, through the dying
tree. The curve reaches, our way
of intersecting at a gallop, and sweetly shapes
a blindness, or a fall.
We balance on the arc, we decide, we
lean into its forgiving hollow.

WINTER

The moon so bright tonight
that three crows flying low cast
shadows like scythes
through the cornfield
they gleaned months back. The road

is dirt-familiar. Fences I know
post by post stretch out
their strange new selves
on the ground. The pines creak
overhead, smoke-soft. Out here,

no one around,
I sing a little and heat
fills my throat. I love my boots,
slap of rubber on calf. I love how
the song never cracks, for once.

I want to walk on and on, keep
going as if no house
were waiting, no friend stood
by the kitchen window, heating
something in a small saucepan.

A car down on the main road turns,
headlights butt against the hill,
fall back. The crows pass down
a gully of air. Cold sloshes
in my boots, has me turning,

taking back every footprint I cut
black into the white frost.

BLUE HERON

Once when we were about to move again,
they got us out of bed in the dark,
drove an hour to the blinds and we waited
to see the herons wake and fly.
Through the trees along the river
ragged gray light came down
like drizzle in the cold,
and we huddled on a log half-sunk in mud.

I had thought a Great Blue Heron would glow
like turquoise but saw just a clothespin
clamped to a poplar. Mom and Dad crouched
on their haunches, lifted the finger for silence.
Finally a folded bird, asleep or lame,
leaned right off its branch,
wings unraveling upward as it came on.
"Oh, Daddy, it's falling!" But the clumsy pennants

caught the air, pulled and held. The crippled neck
unfurled and the sickening legs that flapped drew in
as it rose and rose
and rowed away.
Then more birds on their perches
wavered and dove, one by one dropped
from the parapet of trees. Looking worn,
they pedaled out, pivoted, and became for a while

weightless and blue. Slooping down,
they pinned the river's edges,
long beaks parried the waxy waves.
And we began to watch everything:
the way they jabbed and ate,

our father's wide hands, the black thermos cup
our mother filled, the bristling nests.
I don't remember leaving
or the long drive back through traffic,

or the move west, farther and farther
from the place we thought was home. Maybe
the heron day was one of the last
blessings. Right when it was time
to take an interest in the world of men,
they pointed past it, saying, "Look—what flies."

ABOUT THE WORD WORKS

The Word Works, a nonprofit literary organization, publishes contemporary poetry in collectors' editions. Since 1981, the organization has sponsored the Washington Prize, a $1,500 award to an American poet. Monthly, The Word Works presents free literary programs in the Chevy Chase, MD, Café Muse series, and each summer, free poetry programs are held at the historic Joaquin Miller Cabin in Washington, DC's Rock Creek Park. Annually, two high school students debut in the Miller Cabin Series as winners of the Jacklyn Potter Young Poets Competition.

Since 1974, Word Works programs have included: "In the Shadow of the Capitol," a symposium and archival project on the African-American intellectual community in segregated Washington, DC; the Gunston Arts Center Poetry Series (Ai, Carolyn Forché, and Stanley Kunitz, among others); the Poet-Editor panel discussions at the Writer's Center (John Hollander, Maurice English, Anthony Hecht, Josephine Jacobsen, and others); and Master Class workshops (Agha Shahid Ali, Thomas Lux, Marilyn Nelson).

In 2010, The Word Works will have published 70 titles, including past work from such authors as Deirdra Baldwin, J.H. Beall, Christopher Bursk, John Pauker, Edward Weismiller, and Mac Wellman. Currently, The Word Works publishes books and occasional anthologies under three imprints: the Washington Prize, the Hilary Tham Capital Collection, and International Editions. Information on Toad Hall Editions, a publishing division of The Word Works, can be seen at ToadHallMedia.com.

Past grants to The Word Works have been awarded by the National Endowment for the Arts, National Endowment for the Humanities, DC Commission on the Arts & Humanities, Witter Bynner Foundation, Writer's Center, Bell Atlantic, Batir Foundation, and others, including many generous private patrons.

The Word Works has established an archive of artistic and administrative materials in the Washington Writing Archive housed in the George Washington University Gelman Library.

The Word Works PO Box 42164 Washington, DC 20015
editor@wordworksdc.com   www.wordworksdc.com

OTHER WORD WORKS BOOKS

Washington Prize-winning books

Nathalie F. Anderson, *Following Fred Astaire* (1998)
Michael Atkinson, *One Hundred Children Waiting for a Train* (2001)
Carrie Bennett, *biography of water* (2004)
Peter Blair, *Last Heat* (1999)
Richard Carr, *Ace* (2008)
Ann Rae Jonas, *A Diamond Is Hard But Not Tough* (1997)
Frannie Lindsay, *Mayweed* (2009)
Richard Lyons, *Fleur Carnivore* (2005)
Fred Marchant, *Tipping Point* (1993)
Ron Mohring, *Survivable World* (2003)
Jay Rogoff, *The Cutoff* (1994)
Prartho Sereno, *Call from Paris* (2007)
Enid Shomer, *Stalking the Florida Panther* (1985)
John Surowiecki, *The Hat City after Men Stopped Wearing Hats* (2006)
Miles Waggener, *Phoenix Suites* (2002)

Hilary Tham Capital Collection

Mel Belin, *Flesh That Was Chrysalis*
Doris Brody, *Judging the Distance*
Sarah Browning, *Whiskey in the Garden of Eden*
Christopher Conlon, *Gilbert and Garbo in Love*
    Mary Falls: Requiem for Mrs. Surratt
Donna Denizé, *Broken Like Job*
James Hopkins, *Eight Pale Women*
Brandon Johnson, *Love's Skin*
Judith McCombs, *The Habit of Fire*
Kathi Morrison-Taylor, *By the Nest*
Miles David Moore, *The Bears of Paris*
    Rollercoaster
Maria Terrone, *The Bodies We Were Loaned*
Hilary Tham, *Bad Names for Women*
    Counting
Jonathan Vaile, *Blue Cowboy*
Rosemary Winslow, *Green Bodies*

INTERNATIONAL EDITIONS

Yoko Danno & James C. Hopkins, *The Blue Door*
Moshe Dor, Barbara Goldberg, Giora Leshem, eds., *The Stones Remember*
Myong-Hee Kim, *Crow's Eye View: The Infamy of Lee Sang, Korean Poet*
Vladimir Levchev, *Black Book of the Endangered Species*

ADDITIONAL TITLES

Karren L. Alenier, Hilary Tham, Miles David Moore, eds., *Winners: A Retrospective of the Washington Prize*
Jacklyn Potter, Dwaine Rieves, Gary Stein, eds. *Cabin Fever: Poets at Joaquin Miller's Cabin*
Robert Sargent, *Aspects of a Southern Story*
A Woman From Memphis

ABOUT THE COVER ART

The encaustic panel, "Frog," comes from the multi-media studio of Anastasia Nute in Cambridge, N.Y. She says, "Wax, the encaustic medium, allows me to use layer upon layer, removing at will—revealing what is hidden as the story evolves." She has been mesmerized by color since she was seven, when she discovered a trunk full of art materials in an old shed. That shed became her first studio, and she has worked in many media ever since.